YOUR KNOWLEDGE HAS VALUE

- We will publish your bachelor's and master's thesis, essays and papers

- Your own eBook and book - sold worldwide in all relevant shops

- Earn money with each sale

Upload your text at www.GRIN.com and publish for free

Bibliographic information published by the German National Library:

The German National Library lists this publication in the National Bibliography; detailed bibliographic data are available on the Internet at http://dnb.dnb.de .

Imprint:

Copyright © 2018 GRIN Verlag
Print and binding: Books on Demand GmbH, Norderstedt Germany
ISBN: 9783346101785

This book at GRIN:

https://www.grin.com/document/505851

Moniruzzaman Kiron

Benefits and Drawbacks of Retail's Retention and Acquisition Strategy

Comparison of Watson Company and Guardian Company

GRIN Verlag

GRIN - Your knowledge has value

Since its foundation in 1998, GRIN has specialized in publishing academic texts by students, college teachers and other academics as e-book and printed book. The website www.grin.com is an ideal platform for presenting term papers, final papers, scientific essays, dissertations and specialist books.

Visit us on the internet:

http://www.grin.com/

http://www.facebook.com/grincom

http://www.twitter.com/grin_com

Table of Contents

Introduction

Retention and acquisition strategy of Watson store

Several acquisitions and retention strategy have identified this Watson Company in Australia. This company became the 5th largest company in this country.

Acquisition strategy of Watson Store,

1. Incentive speaking: The statement contained on press release refers to Watson's estimation and future result with non-historical facts. Statements reflect the current perspective on existing information and trends as per releasing data. This firm announced on acquiring Ascent in Southeast Asia and Australia on pharmaceutical business in cash (Al-Alak, 2014). Acquisition result in Watson became fifth largest on revenue in the UK. Broad portfolio is on Ascent market of brands, generics, OTC products approx 14% with market share. This company also has stated on expanding international operations (commercial) geographic for capitalising existing participate and assets in emerging markets and growing markets. Aus Dollar is of 12 billion with a growth rate of 8%.

2. Advertisement: It might help Watson company to promote their services in the market. It also helps the consumer to understand their types of services and benefits from it.

3. Celebrity endorsement: Increasing the consumer base in a fast way for growing Pharma brand. Consumer retention helps to prove somewhat difficult not for acquiring new ones (Beck, Chapman & Palmatier, 2015). Consumer acquisition for this concern firm provides subtle advertising with the endorsement of a celebrity. This might help to reach out for new clients through various channels. Experiences and services are both included on this channels for this company. Medicine advertising on theory scares for new consumers featuring current celebrity that might do without even noticing Webster and Ilicic. The endorsement has around the advertising that begun and become the norm for placement of high-profile figure on real differences. Sales and brand's reputation on this differences has included. Celebrity endorsed pharmacy help brand might attain on new clients just as per their interest in celebrity used products. It also enables acquiring brand towards loyal consumers through celebrity who support these ventures (Bilgihan & Bujisic, 2015). Clients wanted to take part of it and wanted to meet with them also.

4. Engagement in social media: Facebook, Youtube, Linkedin, Twitter are helpful sites for this company to promote this company's services. Several clients (old and new) might be attracted towards this approach of the company, and special discounting offer on their services might make them take the facilities. *[Referred to appendix 1]*

Factors of retention strategy of Watson Ltd,

1. Loyalty program: Corporate efforts (promotional) might attract a new consumer for the business. Retaining consumers help to build establishment and marketing success of Watson Company. Ongoing analysis services and reporting provide feedback on the allowing target and marketing campaigns more effectively. Advanced management database services complement provide and retention strategy effectively (Giannakis, Harker & Baum, 2015). Data hygiene, storage, reduplication are the marketing approach. Integrating services might be related and new email addresses for reducing waste bandwidth and e-mails.

2. Dialogue: Watson Company is currently looking on redefining performance ratings of the employee. These have considered the best way of assessing performances, surveys, to show often disengagement factors for the employees, managers to prevent from transparent dialogue (undertaking). This dialogue takes place twice over the year.

3. Consumer service: This firm is recently reducing attrition, selling, communication calendar (frequently), consumer services (extraordinary), Courtesy system, service integrity, lifestyle measuring value and many more.

4. Referrals: Watson Company listed on the podcasts; build trust, cost-effective towards client for benefits. Client's referral become cost-effective helps to earn a profit, limiting request, showing gratitude from using referrals (Huang, 2015).

Retention strategy and acquisition strategy of the competitors

Factors in Acquisition strategy,

1. Incentive speaking: Guardian Services family Anaheim might benefit from local autonomy model business. This unique model ensures local team to focus on the client's service for meeting specific needs on residents and communities. Corporate assists team in time-consuming business operation day-to-day included HR, IT, Payroll and more. 30 pharmacies of guardian family together serve 100,000 residents and 20 states.

2. Advertisement: As Linkedin became a valuable network for the B2B marketers, this company has chosen this area for advertising the product.

Connecting with the clients, prospects for remotely business done with on the LinkedIn help to increase the business (Hwang & Kandampully, 2015).

3. Celebrity endorsement: This Company is currently not looking for any celebrity to market their products. The belief of their selling strategy is genuine and customer choices based. Opening up large pool for online shoppers sometimes end up existing consumer about current market offerings from Guardian. Shoppers with three devices have used for making a purchase. Direct selling without any celebrity is the primary strategy for this company.

4. Engagement in social media: Increasing people number engaging and reading with emails for sending subscriber list through targeting people who have failed on opening them. 48 hours of sending email for subscription with increasing open numbers campaign inboxes with the same email. Increasing with 35.4% rate of total numbers email and 39% increase on click-through rate (Miquel-Romero, Caplliure-Giner & Adame-Sánchez, 2014). Guardian company also increase organic traffic search with the commercial intent through keywords for specific location and industry as per the company's target. Feature-specific and location specific pages are the current facilities for this company. This company also acquire website with content migrate with keyword rankings. Proper scope and list of several websites help this company to maintain a considerable number of the client database.

Factors in retention strategy are,

1. Loyalty program: Successful brand such as Guardian products provides establishment of an effective retention strategy. Investing brands on consumer loyalty might help retention and drive engagement to attract consumer through simple design program on real appeal and consumer (Ryu & Lee, 2017).

2. Dialogue: Managing dialogue with partnerships (intrinsic-extrinsic) might be useful in solving solutions to the problem. The proper developing dialogue might prevent failure between the two.

3. Consumer service: The underestimate power on loyal base consumer according to Guardian, 15% of consumers are loyal towards single retailer and increase 70% sale. Retaining consumer provides critical aspects of the business (Samaha, Beck & Palmatier, 2014).

4. Referrals: Reducing cost is the main referrals for this company.

Comparison between the retail company and its competitor

Objectives (Total outlets): Watson with 105 stores and Guardian 154 stores.

Social media: Watson has 157K+ views and likes, having Instagrams and twitter account, having one website and Guardian has 45K+ likes and views, no such accounts, having more than two websites.

Membership benefits: Watson has member card with $5 and Guardian has Golden Card (seniors), Passion card.

Exclusive products: Watson has Cosmetics, Brigitte, Skincare, Bio-essence, Derma, Beauty Biotics Haircare, Oral supplements, Beauty gadgets and Guardian has Skincare, Rodial, Skincode, Bioderma, Haircare as their exclusive products.

Analysis: Several differences are found from the upper table after doing a proper analysis. A total outlet of Watson Company in Australia is having 105 stores whereas Guardian company has 154 stores in Australia. Social media usage popularity is for Watson having over 157K likings on social media such as Facebook. Proper Instagram and Twitter account is having almost the same number of views for this company. Guardian company is having over 45K likings and views on Facebook through this company does not use any Instagrams and Twitter account. Watson Company has one single website for operation whereas Guardian company has more than 3 websites for operation. Membership benefits for Watson Company provide $5 member card, and Guardian company provides Golden Card (seniors) with passion card as a membership card (Samiee, Chabowski & Hult, 2015).

Cosmetic products of Watson renowned are for smart, fun, affordable makeup to create a cache for lives and colour. Working colour through presenting individual on the vast array is with wearable colours and brightest in innovative and vibrant packaging at the unbeatable prices. Brigitte originated cosmetics from a country as Japan created through Vivi, Rola, and ex-pop teen model. Aiming at helping girls to transform from ordinary into the Kawaii goddesses with few steps simplify. Brigitte provides ideal content for the sassy women, confident constantly on-the-go with a wide array of unique makeup and natural products. SunKiller carries with a wide range of products which might pretty on consumer needs from active and sporty individuals with skin dry and offerings items for the babies.

Award-winning and consumer favourite facial brand, body care, eye have always forefront with innovation developing products helping on maintaining and achieving healthy skin. Dermatology brand cosmetics has founded science*innovation approach with skincare with its improvement of products with immediate results and efficiency. Sun Enterprises provides manufacturing FDA-approved and ISO-certified beauty equipment over 20 years with six continents. Guardian company boots beauty brand and health partnered on beauty and health on selling products exclusively for Australia. On December 2013, these nine available selections provided Guardian stores. Boots might go over the 500 products hugely with range, hair care, and plant-rich skin from Botanics, extract boots, dermocare, professional salon products from the luxurious and Mark Hill treats Chimneys. Swiss-based brand skincare skin code first launched through this company in 2014. Dermatologically product tasting with patented grade-ingredient reduces accelerates and ageing skin recovery. Another product of this company has provided such as Vitagreen, back joy, sleep Ezy are the essential products for this Guardian company (guardianpharmacies.com.au, 2018). *[Referred to appendix 2]*

Discuss the benefits and drawbacks of retail's retention and acquisition strategy

Several drawback and benefits have provided in this study for acquisition and retention strategy on both the company. Benefits such as,

a. Retention usually viewed securing revenues in a practical way (cost) with product differentiation function, specific industry and switching costs parameters. Successful incumbent needs for smartly leverages on creating retention program with increasing loyalty on lowest cost. Consumer acquisition has positioned with competitive project acquisition. However, this acquisition costs provide high retention through associated benefits analysis. Benefit for acquisition need is fully quantified with accurate relative gauge value on each approach.

b. Very often found on getting business of every bit with the existing base for constant on ensuring all parts of this business. Network on existing with full consumer believe several companies to become forget and complacent for appreciation on consumer goods. Need of making consumer feelings have proactive and appreciated on those with new. (Watsonpharmacy, 2018)

c. Consumer became more demanding to grow competition to get about more choices. The need for innovative and new ways to satisfy and retain consumers cannot underestimate from the competitors. Unique and different keeping ways for competition, consumers might acquire the same. Consumer acquisition provides the necessity for both companies. Growth with unique benefits experienced through both the companies with the retention rates have provided. Profits might improve considerably during consumers board stay with an extended period. Acquiring the cost of putting and consumer books runs four times for annual cost. Longer keeping all clients of this company for several years for one-time costs of spreading, Sheridan. Marketing and sales together retain and acquire profitable consumers. Following Al-

Alak, (2014), supported through recent discussion on Linkedin with significant differences for marketing and sales with proper trends of using short-term revenue emphasis might profitable long run focusing. Connecting with the profitability and retention over time might spend with consumer attraction with well define consumer retention strategy. The cost might provide 10 times on acquiring consumer for keeping existing consumer for marketing budget allocation with the acquisition. Les attention might provide existing consumer retention to spend money on marketing and communication for consumer acquisition.

Recommendation

Recommendation 1: (Data for integration): Every business might not rely on existence consumer market share and goodwill that Watson enjoys during Watson enjoys multichannel offerings for living up expectations. An executive might want on staying channel focusing awarding with optimising limitations in the channels. The moderate majority on advance marketing still integrate across the channels. Watson skews heavily on unintegrated activities with focused-channel. Several impacts on focusing channel seen an organisation that might see quite advancement in understandings digital transformation and journeys. Both the companies have mentioned high-profitable failings with the delivery operation and call centre. Delivery choice services became damaged during past work experiences for Watson. Multichannel organising understandings with consumer choices might able to provide meetings on involving markets. Operations, sales and merchandising insight might provide unique positioning on brand with its services for both the companies. Cost-driven outsourcing put inventory and handling management through tide growing complaints.

Recommendation 2: (Mobile as a platform): Mobile app and website generated 16% respondents respectively. Apps continue scoring low expectation still wrestling investment with branded apps. Consumer mobile interaction with social apps helps to share of the mind. Watson has experienced decline fortunes in Australia over two past decades. Revenue might up through 0.5% a year with establishment stores with proper footfall. One contributing factors introduced Watson payment through this app for becoming a powerful offline integration tool (multi-channel) in the future. Watson's app on 22m monthly users with online orders comes through proper way. Integrating function app might use of storing QR code is similar to Watson versions. Usage of mobile m-commerce with essential function is delivering experiences with the enabler. Provide enabling a consumer with essential function multichannel delivering experiences with the enabler. The consumer provides reached experiences to integrate functionalities to prove go-transportation and convenient. This might ease delivering services for both the companies. 31% responses remain important point towards consumer journey during consumer acquisition. Both companies might careful on the approaches with search strategies for proper viewing. Organic search might provide brand mercy recognition to consider paid implication searching results on the first page. A company might invest to build recognition and awareness on making proper searching more effectively (cost) with expensive generic keyword pushing with the top result.

Conclusion

This study has concluded about Watson Pharmacy in Australia which is one of the reputed companies in this country. Proper retention and acquisition strategy of this company has adequately provided. Incentives speak, advertisement, engaging social media, endorsement are the part of the acquisition strategy. Loyalty program, Consumer services, referrals are the factors of retention strategy of this company. Guardian store is the main rival company for Watson, and proper comparison has provided. Proper benefit discussion on retention and Watson strategy have provided suitably after analysis proper recommendations have appropriately provided to improve this company's sales. Hence, proper marketing relation might help to increase the business growth of this company in the future.

Reference list

Journals

Al-Alak, B. A. (2014). Impact of marketing activities on relationship quality in the Malaysian banking sector. *Journal of Retailing and Consumer Services, 21*(3), 347-356. Retrieved from: https://www.hamyarprojeh.ir/wp-content/uploads/2016/10/wwww.hamyarprojeh.ir-English-3835-1.pdf, Retrieved on 9.11.2018

Beck, J. T., Chapman, K., & Palmatier, R. W. (2015). Understanding relationship marketing and loyalty program effectiveness in global markets. *Journal of International Marketing, 23*(3), 1-21. Retrieved from: https://research-repository.griffith.edu.au/bitstream/handle/10072/337614/BeckPUB2511.pdf?sequenc e=1&isAllowed=y, Retrieved on 4.11.2018

Bilgihan, A., & Bujisic, M. (2015). The effect of website features in online relationship marketing: A case of online hotel booking. *Electronic Commerce Research and Applications, 14*(4), 222-232., Retrieved from https://s3.amazonaws.com/academia.edu.documents/36282881/e_commerce_research .pdf?AWSAccessKeyId=AKIAIWOWYYGZ2Y53UL3A&Expires=1542865164&Si gnature=d3HFhg%2FSoQDEnKlTOTdZCCLm6Ec%3D&response-content-disposition=inline%3B%20filename%3DThe_effect_of_website_features_in_online.p df, Retrieved on 1.11.2018

Giannakis, D., Harker, M. J., & Baum, T. (2015). Human resource management, services and relationship marketing: the potential for cross-fertilisation. *Journal of Strategic Marketing, 23*(6), 526-542. Retrieved from: https://strathprints.strath.ac.uk/53137/1/Harker_etal_JSM_2015_Human_resource_ma nagement_services_and_relationship_marketing.pdf, Retrieved on 10.11.2018

Huang, M. H. (2015). The influence of relationship marketing investments on customer gratitude in retailing. *Journal of Business Research, 68*(6), 1318-1323. Retrieved from: http://iranarze.ir/wp-content/uploads/2016/07/4496-English.pdf, Retrieved on: 6.11.2018

Hwang, J., & Kandampully, J. (2015). Embracing CSR in pro-social relationship marketing program: understanding driving forces of positive consumer responses. *Journal of Services Marketing, 29*(5), 344-353. from: https://www.researchgate.net/profile/Jay_Kandampully/publication/282054960_Embr acing_CSR_in_pro-social_relationship_marketing_program_Understanding_driving_forces_of_positive_consumer_responses/links/5836146808ae503ddbb3938a/Embracing-CSR-in-pro-social-relationship-marketing-program-Understanding-driving-forces-of-positive-consumer-responses.pdf, Retrieved on: 7.11.2018

Miquel-Romero, M. J., Caplliure-Giner, E. M., & Adame-Sánchez, C. (2014). Relationship marketing management: Its importance in private label extension. *Journal of Business Research, 67*(5), 667-672. Retrieved from: http://www.isihome.ir/freearticle/ISIHome.ir-22088.pdf, Retrieved on: 8.11.2018

Ryu, K., & Lee, J. S. (2017). Examination of restaurant quality, relationship benefits, and customer reciprocity from the perspective of relationship marketing investments. *Journal of Hospitality & Tourism Research, 41*(1), 66-92., Retrieved from: https://journals.sagepub.com/doi/pdf/10.1177/1096348013515919, Retrieved on: 3.11.2018

Samaha, S. A., Beck, J. T., & Palmatier, R. W. (2014). The role of culture in international relationship marketing. *Journal of Marketing, 78*(5), 78-98. Retrieved from: https://research-repository.griffith.edu.au/bitstream/handle/10072/337608/SamahaPUB2497.pdf?sequ ence=1&isAllowed=y, Retrieved on: 2.11.2018

Samiee, S., Chabowski, B. R., & Hult, G. T. M. (2015). International relationship marketing: Intellectual foundations and avenues for further research. *Journal of International Marketing, 23*(4), 1-21. Retrieved from: https://www.researchgate.net/profile/Tomas_Hult/publication/281388890_Internation al_Relationship_Marketing_Intellectual_Foundations_and_Avenues_for_Future_Rese arch/links/56a25e4308aef91c8c0ee831.pdf, Retrieved on: 5.11.2018,

Websites

guardianpharmacies.com.au (2018), *guardianpharmacies*, Available at: https://www.guardianpharmacies.com.au/ (Accessed on: 15.11.2018)

watsonpharmacy (2018), *watsonpharmacy*, Available at: http://watsonpharmacy.com.au/ (Accessed on: 14.11.2018)

Appendices

Appendix1: Marketing strategy

Figure 5: BD&AA suffers from a lack of clear responsibilities and ownership, with many respondents citing multiple answers
Who owns your company data strategy?

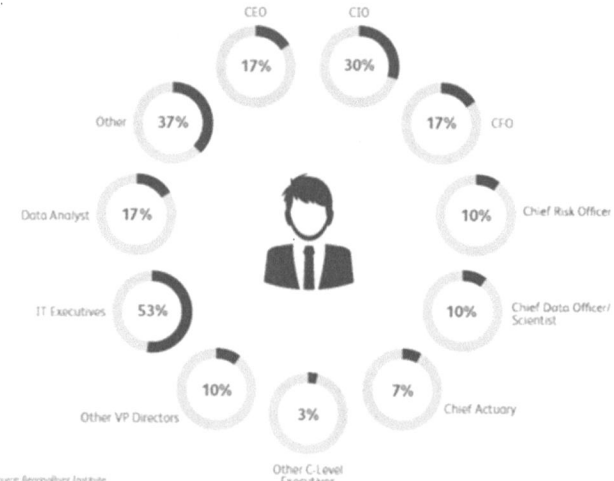

(Source: https://www.bearingpoint.com/en/our-success/thought-leadership/the-smart-insurer-embedding-big-data-in-corporate-strategy/)